CONVENT OF SANTA MARIA LA REAL DE HUELGAS, BURGOS

Editorial Everest, S.A. are grateful to all the members of the National Heritage who collaborated in the production of this book.

Translated by: Susan Gosling

Photographs: Foto Santi (Burgos)

Layout: Gerardo Rodera

Carretera León-La Coruña, km 5 - LEON
ISBN: 84-241-4990-4
Legal Deposit: LE. 1.001 - 1991
Printed in Spain

EDITORIAL EVERGRAFICAS, S. A.
Carretera León-La Coruña, km 5
LEON (Spain)

CONVENT OF SANTA MARIA LA REAL DE HUELGAS, BURGOS

FRAY VALENTIN DE LA CRUZ
College of Fine Arts
Official Chronicler of the Province of Burgos

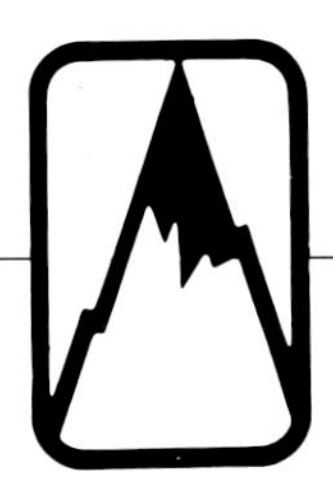

EDITORIAL EVEREST, S. A.

MADRID • LEON • BARCELONA • SEVILLA • GRANADA • VALENCIA
ZARAGOZA • LAS PALMAS DE GRAN CANARIA • LA CORUÑA
PALMA DE MALLORCA • ALICANTE – MEXICO • BUENOS AIRES

CONVENT OF SANTA MARIA LA REAL DE HUELGAS, BURGOS

I. Opening Thoughts

Travellers:

You have completed the journey to Burgos, Capital of Castile. You have come from lands near or far and your steps have been illuminated with the illusion of walking, seeing and discovering. Following the River Arlanzón that flows beside the road to Valladolid, through lands that once were vegetable gardens and fine pasturelands (hence the name «Huelgas», or unsown land), you have arrived at this place, born eight centuries ago, nestling beside a convent.

And now you are, we are, beside this fine fountain whose water is a banner of jubilation and an invitation to jubilation. We are standing in the «Compás de Adentro». In old Spanish «compás» meant the portico, the courtyard or reserved space before the door of monasteries, convents and churches. In this «compás» doors open up and buildings of diverse styles and destinies converge: the Renaissance entrance to the convent; the rectilineal residences of the high officials and the attested chaplains of the former abbatial domain; a Gothic tower; a Gothic passageway to the Compás de Afuera (outer courtyard), and the buttresses at the front of the church, as simple as the bare feet of a pilgrim.

But it is not a good idea to rush straight into the building that awaits us. The traveller who has come this far with expectant spirit and his eyes open deserves, and perhaps needs, some previous reflection, a mental approximation to the truths that are about to surround him. That way the result will be more enjoyable, and these stones and this blue light, the silence of the sepulchres and the prayers of the nuns, the pieces of art and the shreds of history will fulfil the reason for which they were united: to be understood and remembered as a whole.

The visitor must remember that this is first and foremost a convent. It is a point of religious seriousness. Do not be dazzled by misleading publicity or by the exclusive artistic appearances or other expressions. Here everything is conceived, carried out, conserved, led, vitalized by a community or congregation of women dedicated to ideals which may differ widely from our own, but

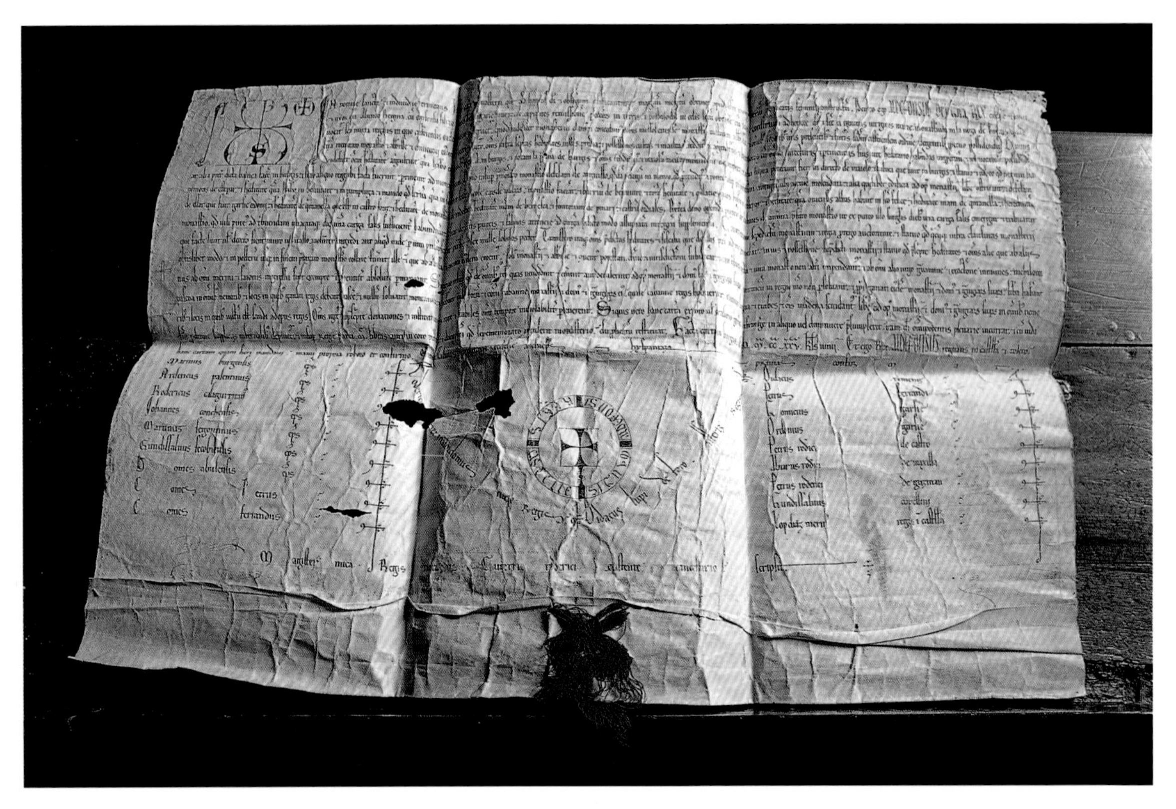

1. *Foundation document by Alfonso VIII (1187). Convent Archives.*

which in this place are completely inherent and eternal.

These words become evident before the fact, now based on eight centuries of reality, of the continued devotion. From 1187 to these days the same spirit has encouraged the nuns to voluntarily enclose themselves behind these walls. Still alive is the will of Alfonso VIII, the founding king: «We will construct, to the honour of God and His holy mother, the Virgin Mary, a convent in the lowlands of Burgos, which will be called Santa María la Real and where the Cistercian Rule will be observed».

Pope Clement III took the first abbess, Doña Misol, and her community under his direct protection and declared: «First we establish that the conventual life, which is declared to have been set up acccording to God and the Rule of St. Benedict and the Institutions of the Cistercian Order, will be observed for all time, inviolably, in the same place...».

This convent belongs to the Cistercian Order, an almost legendary spiritual and social movement which was established in the north of France at the beginning of the 12th century and filled the holy building and history of Europe in the following centuries, led by the great, admirable figure of St. Bernard of Clairvaux. Its banner was the Rule of St. Benedict, the patron saint of Europe, interpreted with certain literary criteria which converted the Cistercians into singers of divine praise as well as cultivators of barren land to sustain themselves with food produced using their own hands.

The Cistercians also added to the admirable Benedictine Rule what is known as a *Chapter of Charity*, which characterises the life of the members of the Order and of its abbeys and monasteries, which are set apart from the rest of the world, and demands norms and manners that are completely different from those practised outside its cloisters. The visiting hours to these and the rest of the convent are concessions on behalf of the nuns to the legitimate desire of those people who come here to discover a home of transcedental and cultural representations which are as varied as they are interesting.

Since the above-mentioned year of 1187 a white constellation (their choral habits are white) of Cistercian nuns has tried to be faithful to their retreat, prayer, liturgy and manual work. That secular spirit has impregnated the walls and the atmosphere: it has cristalised the psalmody and if one day it ever made the nuns stop singing the very air would be filled with Gregorian chants. This means that we must have the courtesy to keep our options and opinions to ourselves, so as better to capture the spirit of this place.

Among the nuns who live within this convent one figure moves and stands out, sailing between the seas of myth and reality: that of the abbess. There is a long abundance of literature about her, with comments and delightful sayings. What was the abbess really like? How much truth is there in the historical account? For indeed, the question is about the past, as the present is so plain and so simple that it is outstanding in grandeur and religiousness. In fact, the abbesses of our times are only responsible for the usufruct, as since the last century

2. *Clement III's papal bull.*

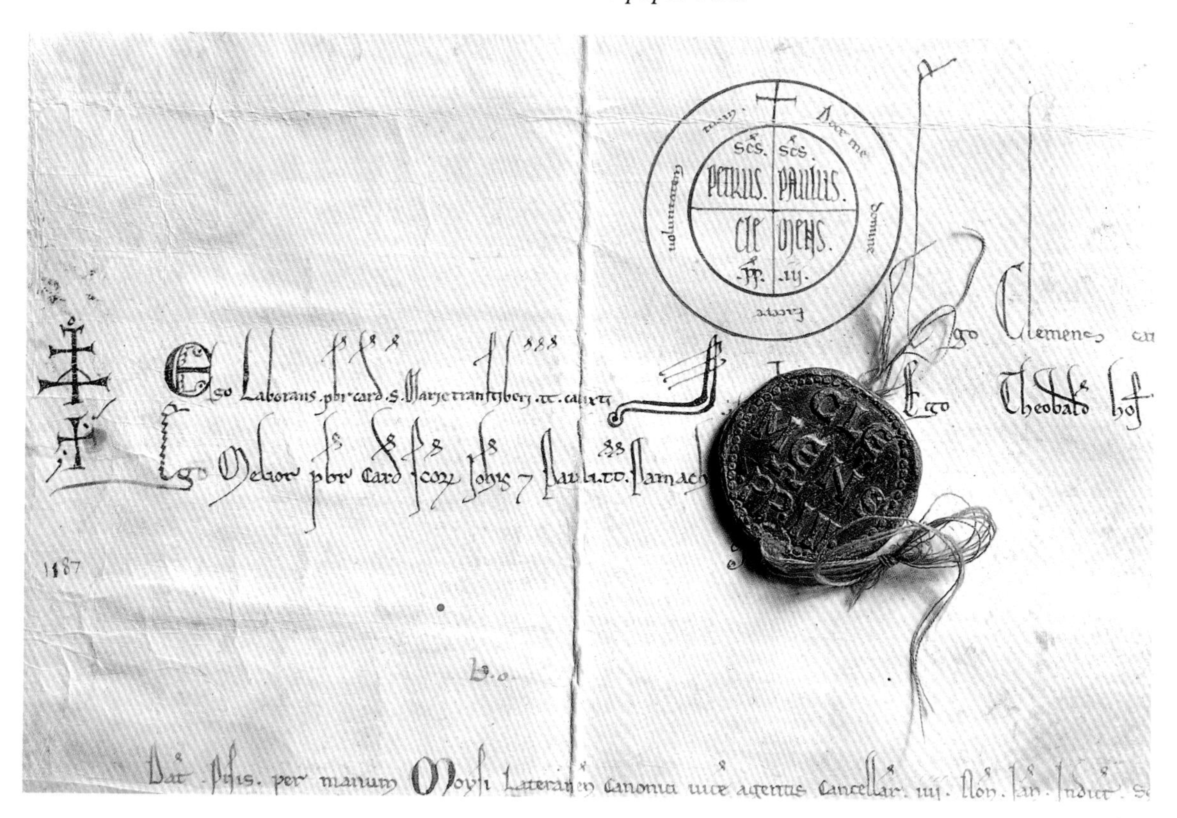

this convent has belonged to the National Heritage, and all that concerns this royal and religious place is looked after by the said body with special meticulousness. The patron is still His Majesty the King of Spain.

At the end of the 19th century, just before the elimination of private jurisdiction in the Church, the abbess of Santa María la Real still began her orders and decrees in the following way: «We, Doña..., by the grace of God and the Holy Apostolic See, abbess of the Real Monasterio de las Huelgas, near the city of Burgos, of the Cistercian Order, Order of our Father St. Bernard, Owner, Superior, Prelate, Mother and lawful administrator of all spiritual and material in the said Convent and its Hospital, called Hospital del Rey, and of the convents, churches and chapels under her control by virtue of apostolic bulls and concessions, with absolute and cuasi episcopal jurisdiction *nullius diocesis...»*.

This statement, which causes admiration among experts in the history of law as it is unusual, is a result of a series of causes. This convent, constructed by order of monarchs, was started with determined purposes, the fulfilment of which the monarchs wanted to ensure with the same element as supported it: power. Santa María la Real was designed to be a reflection of the Crown and had to be endowed with some monarchical similarities both in people and in things.

In small proportions Huelgas in Burgos had to be a theocratic state within a political state, and its head had to appear to be invested with independence and powers. For this reason King Alfonso VIII and Queen Eleanor broke 49 towns and villages off their kingdom and handed them over with full and absolute powers, by order of the supreme authority of the Crown. To this the Pope added that «absolute, cuasi episcopal» jurisdiction over the vassals within these material domains.

In this way a woman, a unique case in Western civil and clerical life, governed her isle with no interference apart from that of the king or the Pope. Justice was administered in her name; she held audiences and had a prison; she imposed and charged tributes and controlled the accounts; exonerated sins, performed marriage services, gave authority to her priests, gave powers to her own father confessor, appointed parish priests and distributed parishes. No other authority, be it a bishop, visitor, local governor, corregidor or investigating judge could override the abbess's material or spiritual powers, and other abbesses courted her.

The visitor is surely wondering. And why was this? How did it come about? The figure whom we are presenting was not born spontaneously or without due thought. In fact, there had been two impressive precedents in the very same land of Castile. The apanage-abbacy of Covarrubias, founded by Count García Fernández in 978 in the name of his young daughter Urraca, and the seigniorial abbacy of San Salvador de Oña, established by Count Sancho in the name of his daughter Tigridia in 1011.

This situation was sought after and obtained by the founding monarchs, and the ecclesiastical and civil society accepted that, although not always with delight and deference. As was mentioned before, the founders were King Alfonso VIII of Castile and his wife Eleanor of England, of the Plantagenet House. We should now assign to each of these his quota of responsibility.

My own particular opinion, deduced, to be honest, from history, concedes the initiative and the more tenacious perseverence in the undertaking to Queen Eleanor. In the

3. *Apse of the convent church.*

4. *The Inner Courtyard.*

Chronicles written by Alfonso X (the Wise), great-grandson of the founders and authoritative student of the secrets of history, wrote the following in his table of the 13th century: «Because of the many petitions and because of the great desire of the very noble Queen Eleanor, his wife, he began to construct and to build near Burgos a convent for the ladies of the Order of Cistercians». And the same Wise king, in a moment of lyrical rapture, abandoned the Spanish language and took up Galician to write this explanatory verse in his «Cantigas»:

«And then (the King) went back to Castile
And there in Burgos he stayed
And built a hospital
He and his wife built
The convent of Las Huelgas».

Queen Eleanor came to Castile when she was changing from childhood to puberty; she had been born in 1160 and arrived in Burgos in 1170. But the conduct of her family was engraved in the eyes of the princess, in particular that of her mother, also called Eleanor, who was calming her haughty spirit with prayer and a quiet life in the Convent of Fontevrault, in English Aquitaine. The family of the new Queen of Castile was rough and terrible. Her father Henry II, had had Thomas à Becket killed in Canterbury Cathedral; her mother was considered a dominant woman and called an intriguer and an «instigator of divorces». Of her brothers, one was Richard the Lionheart and another King John...

Also, for this royal maiden, Fontevrault was something other than a place of retreat and sepulchre for the family. It was the expression of a new concept of women, which was striving to force its way into 12th century society. In Fontevrault an abbess ruled over a large congregation of nuns and monks; she disposed of the money and the people, and the men in the Order respected her decisions. The sermons and writings of Bernard of Clairvaux, the most perfect embellishment of the Cistercians, coincided with these ideas. He augmented the importance of women when he resumed

5. *Gothic arch joining the inner and outer squares.*

the Christian doctrine of the Humanity of God and gave importance to the Virgin Mary as a woman capable of assuming responsabilities. Romanesque society felt a breath of feminism under its skin, and authorised ladies to preside over tournaments, and queens to lead courts of jongleurs and minstrels.

Eleanor, who adhered to this spirit of feminism, felt able to create in her adopted country a strength which would place a woman in the right place to be a mother, informer and leader. When she tried to realise these abstractions Eleanor confronted everybody and had to animate her own husband's inertia, overcome the educated resistance of the leaders of the Church (all men), and, especially, change the opinion of the Cistercian monks among whom there was stubborn opposition to the acceptation of convents in their order. What you are now going to visit proves that Eleanor overcame everybody.

Is the visitor convinced? There will be time as we go round to repeat the facts and offer some more. As you now know where and when this happened, let us move on.

II. The Exterior

The various buildings that can be seen (the church, convent, houses, towers, outer wall etc.) were built at different times. All this, as well as the following district, rose

6. *Apses of the church and the chapel of San Juan.*

up on wide, lush pasture land, where the people from Burgos would let their animals free to «idle», to rest from their hard tasks on the land, to graze on the fine grass and improve their meat and skins. In all the villages in Burgos there were cattle and flocks at rest. This normal human necessity did not prevent the first kings of Castile from building a country mansion or small palace, also with the intention of resting, as we all, animals and men, have need of this, even if the latter be crowned.

The fountain has its own particular charm, especially in the entwined tails of the four fish. Beside the church stands a cross vault with Christ Crucified on one side and the Virgin with Child on the other.

The entrance or lodge of the convent is at the end of the Inner Courtyard; it is protected by a quintuple, semi-circular arcade, in Renaissance style, topped with fine spires and royal coats-of-arms. The Royal Entrance is blocked up and is only opened, by breaking it through, when monarchs of Spain visit the convent. Opposite it the 14th century tower was built; below it was the entrance to the convent buildings.

History has it that at times the monarchs stayed in this tower, and that here was born King Pedro the Cruel (or the Just), who was to finish up so sadly. It was a Tuesday, 30th of August, 1334 and, some say, the queen disposed of a dead daughter for whom she immediately substituted, through a Hebrew maid, a baby born in the house of another Jew, Pedro (Pero) Gil. For this reason King Pedro's followers were known as the «Emperogilados».

The secular dominion of the convent and its abbess was proclaimed from the towers and the high walls topped with battlements and variously illustrated disc-shaped stelae. On the other side of the elegant Gothic arch is the Outer Courtyard with the graceful church showing a fine spiral staircase up to the second floor which houses the bells. The tower is somewhat military, as though it were guarding the House of God, with its strong buttresses topped with small towers and with the finishing touch of the lovely balustrade over machicolation arches.

These courtyards and the road outside are now enlivened by the illusion of the visitors, vast numbers of whom arrive enticed by these walls. In the old days it was chaplains, girls on messages, officials and, at certain times of year, the tenants of the convent who came here. From the places closer to Burgos where the convent owned property the workers came with their tribute, generally in the form of grain. Some came on Our Lady's Feast Day (the 8th), others on St. Michael's Day (the 29th). Within a scene full of noise and colours they checked the weights and the owners and they paid their dues. The countrymen would look at the convent in amazement, really satisfied with their own condition because of the grandeur of the domain from which they rented land, and because it was better to haggle with the abbess's people than with those from the royal tax office.

As time went by more people from Burgos started to spend the day in the land around the convent. This first took off from the Day of the Lord, which has always been the name given to Corpus Christi Day in Burgos. That Thursday was, and is, in this city a «day which shines more the sun itself» and citizens of all kinds throw themselves into homage and fervour. But the next day is that of Curpillos, the same festival but given the diminutive name, out of affection, not because it is any less important. Quite the opposite, the morning celebrations in this courtyard are followed by the great afternoon pilgrimage in the adjoining part called the «Parral». «The whole of Burgos», from the Archbishop and the Captain General to the artisans and schoolchildren, goes to Huelgas; the Archbishop carries the Monstrance of the Lord, the Captain waves the Banner of Las Navas, won on the glorious day of that battle (we shall refer to it later). And the people go along with them, praying, singing, dancing and eating, encouraged by the groups of festival animators from the city, by the music and rockets, by the water sellers and by the dancers who offer their performances to the Holy Sacrament.

We are standing before the apses at the end of the church, below the strong tower. Behind us is the chapel of San Martín, recently restored and probably dedicated to the holy Abbot and Bishop of Sigüenza, from the Finojosa family, who took a highly active part in the first years of the life of

7. *Caballeros Cloisters.*

8. *Chapel of San Juan Bautista.*

9. *Romanesque rose window in the atrium of the church.*

10. *Knights' sepulchres in the atrium of the church.*

this convent. Along the side of the church stands the open arcade of what are known the Caballeros Cloisters; it is composed of two doors and ten twinned arches with capitals in one piece; the capitals show varied decoration. We can see a beautiful closed-off door which formerly led to the chapel of Santa Catalina with its triple arcade, the first in saw-edge form. The cloisters show Gothic fan vaulting.

We go through a 18th century neo-classic door to the atrium, which is lit up on the west wall by a beautiful rose window with double radii and small round arches. This light illuminates two early 13th century sepulchres with figures of the Pantocrator seated in the aureole and flanked by His apostles, below pendant arches, and scenes of death and the soul being carried by angels. One of them shows a very original ciborium made up of six columns; the two in the centre with St. Peter and St. Paul resting on them and the four in the corners with angels holding candles. On the foliage decorated capitals rest the imposts that support several ogival arches with towers and merlons at the top. It is not known to whom these partly deteriorated sepulchres belong.

11. *Main entrance door to the church.*

On the east side, in the apses, is the chapel of San Juan Bautista, which is full of light and fine Gothic work. The entrance offers a highly ornate triple archivolt on the exterior; castles and lions follow the sweep of the arch, rather than figures of saints with their canopies. Now there is no tympanum. The chapel contains four sepulchres, three of which show interesting sculptural work.

These are the one supported by two lions and an eagle, beautifully decorated with eight coats-of-arms and a fleur-de-lys cross; the one standing on two lions, also with eight coats-of-arms and a Christ in majesty in the centre; and, finally, the one decorated with great sobriety with quatrefoil medallions containing early 13th century crosses. The sepulchres we have just described are said to belong to Knight of the Band, but as this Order was set up by Alfonso XI (14th century), we have to suppose they belong to others within the mystical mediaeval circle of knights.

The elegant door, adorned with leaves and showing a slender gable, is a proud expression of the Kingdom of Castile governed by Alfonso VIII, the king whose gilded arms were repeatedly campaigning.

12. *St. Bernard, on the high altar.*

III. In the Church

These are the many apses of the convent church. At the end of the 12th century the master builders worked eagerly on its foundations and walls. Soon they abandoned the early Romanesque design of the tower and other elements and accepted the full implication of the architectural demands of the Cistercian Order. He who best described the principles of architecture of his Order was St. Bernard de Clairvaux, one of the most lucid minds of the century and of great influence in the Europe of his own and following centuries. For St. Bernard Cistercian buildings were to be founded on sobriety and clean lines; their elegance is a result of these two sovereign virtues.

With this in mind the structural plan for this convent was drawn up. The design was large, as a numerous community was envisaged, and a large church was called for if it was to serve as a royal pantheon. Plans were made for five aisles, the first of which being open and running along the Outer Courtyard, and the last being used for the processional cloisters of San Fernando. All the branches of the fine arts were called upon to decorate it, but not with the exuberance of the last phase of Romanesque, in accordance with the sobriety called for by the Cistercians, as yet another reproach to Cluny, the Order of Black Monks.

The height of the church matches its amplitude. When was it built, and by whom? Cistercian churches were generally begun almost half a century after the foundation of

13. *St. Benedict, on the high altar.*

14. *Apse of the convent church.* ▶

15. *Gilded iron pulpit commissioned by Catalina Sarmiento.*

16. *The monumental organ in the church.*

17. *High altar. Niche with a figure of Alfonso VIII.*

18. *High altar. Niche with a figure of Queen Eleanor.*

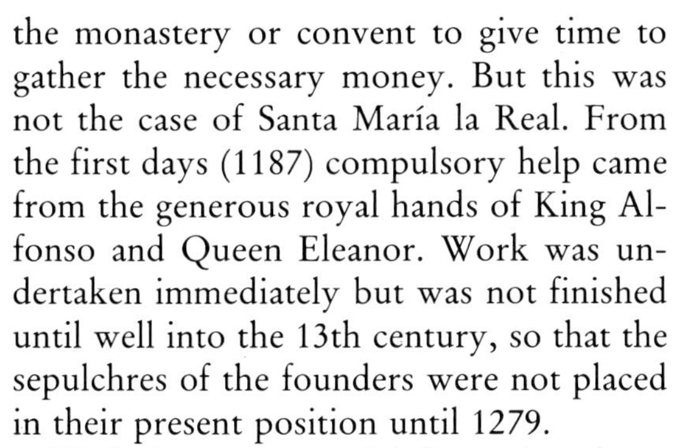

the monastery or convent to give time to gather the necessary money. But this was not the case of Santa María la Real. From the first days (1187) compulsory help came from the generous royal hands of King Alfonso and Queen Eleanor. Work was undertaken immediately but was not finished until well into the 13th century, so that the sepulchres of the founders were not placed in their present position until 1279.

We lack any personal information about the early builders, and only a certain Enrique is mentioned. But there is one unquestionable fact: whoever they were they came from over the Pyrennees, or were influenced by the lastest styles in France and Central Europe. The hand of Angevin can clearly be appreciated in these four absidal chapels. Once again Fontevrault is the source of inspiration. The said chapels are rectangular in shape, but their vaults seem octagonal because of some bevelled arches which join with another coming from the corner, giving the vault a dome-shaped appearance. Solemn, beautiful apses, all the lovelier for lacking altars.

The main aisle, with three sections and vaults showing different divisions, is filled with the splendour and form of the high altarpiece, which is baroque in style. The most famous experts living in Castilla la Vieja at the time –the architect Policarpo de la Nestosa, the sculptor Juan de Pobes and the gilder Pedro Guillén– completed it in 1665. The Virgin Mary begins her ascent to heaven guided by angels, attentively contemplated by St. Benedict (white habit). From their vaulted niches at the sides Alfonso VIII and Queen Eleanor watch and pray; please observe their regalness rather than their clothes, which are not in 13th century style.

19. *Altar of the Presentation of Christ in the transept of the church.*

20. *Apsidal chapel. Christ, by Diego de Siloé (16th century) with Gothic figures.*

On a floor of polished boards stands the choir of the convent chaplains. The stalls show simple work with royal coats-of-arms and jugs of white lillies. In this choir the chaplains fulfilled their liturgical obligations and the canonical hours. These priests were proof of the grandeur of the convent; they lived at its expense and showed obedience to the abbess. The relations between them and the Mother Superior were not always pleasant. One of them did not hesitate to lock all the chaplains up in a tower-cum-prison due to indiscipline within the choir. They were kept on bread and water until their feelings and stomachs got weaker and they begged for pardon. Two passageways were built above the choir stalls, one for the baroque organ and the other for the choristers. Previously the walls were covered with tapestries depicting Biblical and historic scenes (Cain and Abel, Cleopatra).

The transept –we are now standing below its vaults– is soberly conceived and realised; the eight-ribbed vault is also domeshaped, with four bulls eyes to illuminate the scene. Of particular interest in the following chapel, the fourth of the apses, is the Christ Crucified, by Diego de Siloé (16th century); the Virgin Mary and St. John are 13th century, in Gothic style. Visitors should observe the variety of artistic styles that are combined within this church and convent, which break monographic schemes to show the rich variety accumulated over eight centuries.

The fifth chapel has become this sacristy; the entrance door is classic in style. The wall on the southern side of the transept shows a baroque altar with the Presentation of the Virgin Mary in the Temple; the

21. *Painted partition in the central aisle.*

group contains figures by Felipe Vigorny, the Burgundian.

A false wall divides off the western part of the church, separating the section for the congregation and visitors from that reserved for the Cistercian community. The small door that can be seen further to the south was for the nuns' confessor. In the old days, the Cistercian Order had two permanent elderly priests authorised to attend the community spiritually. According to the documents in the archives they were treated very specially.

Let us examine the pulpit, which stands beside the large railing: it revolves so that the nuns can see and hear the preacher better. It was commissioned by Catalina Sarmiento in

1560, a fact that is confirmed by the presence of the 25 coat-of-arms of the family of the abbess. It is in repoussed iron gilded by fire and below scallop-shaped mouldings are figures of Judith, John the Baptist, apostles and so on. Tradition has it that St. Vicente Ferrer preached here, but it should be pointed out, if we are to harmonise tradition with history, that the Valencian saint preached from the pulpit made in walnut wood that stands behind the iron one. So what you are looking at is a reliquary pulpit.

Above the grille, at the top of the partition wall in the central aisle, Jerónimo and Pedro Ruiz de Camargo, the artists from Burgos, offer their own personal vision of the Battle of Las Navas de Tolosa, without paying too much attention to the military realities of 1212. Painted in 1594, the scene must have been well received by the city, as very few years later Pedro was given the task of illustrating the intrados of the Santa María Arch.

Now we must prepare ourselves to enter the inner recess of the convent and visit the manifestations of art housed there. The strict ecclesiastical law of enclosure under which the nuns live is suspended at certain hours on certain days for the benefit of visitors. We will thankfully follow the established route, amazed as we contemplate such things, but never forgetting that we are in a convent belonging to the Cistercian Order.

IV. The Royal Pantheon

This is called the chapel of Santa Catalina. Our attention will first be drawn to the sacorphagi. The funeral intentions of the monarchs on founding this monastery have already been spoken of. It was inevitable for them and one of the demands of their Christian beliefs. King Alfonso and Queen Eleanor knew that death was not the end of the path, that the separation of the body and soul is transitory, that our bodies are dust and to dust they will return in that period of waiting that exists between death and resurrection on the last day. King Alfonso and Queen Eleanor were searching for a sanctified place for themselves and their descendents where their ashes could be moved eternally by the hymns and the psalms of the nuns. When the biblical trumpet sounded they wanted to meet up again with the members of the clergy who had prayed for them and to whom they had donated this convent and all it owned.

Santa María la Real was to be the pantheon in which the family would wait united. Alfonso wanted for Castile what other royal houses in Spain and the rest of Europe already enjoyed: San Isidoro in León, Leyre in Navarre, San Juan de la Peña in Aragón, Ripoll and Poblet in Catalonia, Oña in the part of Castile ruled by counts and Fontevrault in Aquitaine. There is a document in which he explained these intentions: «We promise before the said abbot (of Cistercium) that we, our sons and descendents, if they wish to follow our advice and commands in this matter, we shall be buried in the Convent of Santa María la Real».

This desire of the founders began to be fulfilled before they would have desired it, in the person of their own children. The number of their offspring was cut down with premature deaths that brought into use various sepulchres in both this and other aisles. When Alfonso and Eleanor died in 1214 of all the children they had had only five were with their parents: Berenguela, Constanza, Leonor, Mafalda and Enrique. Urraca was Queen of Portugal and Blanca of France, but three sons called Fernando, two called Sancho, another with the name of Enrique, and two other girls had all died.

22. *Sepulchre of Prince Fernando de la Cerda, Calvary.*

Alfonso and Eleanor's children are like a hieroglyph of numbers, names and dates for historians. Here in this plain stone coffin lies Enrique I, fleetingly King of Castile. He succeeded his parents in 1214, with his eldest sister Berenguela as a very wise regent. The boy-king, unaware of political intrigues, was playing one day with other boys in the courtyard of the residence of the Bishop of Palencia. At one not very precise moment one boy hurt him («against his wishes», say the Chronicles) by hitting his head with a stone, or perhaps the ball they were playing with knocked off a tile which fell upon the royal head. What happened was that they had to carry out a trepanation, which was very well performed by a Jewish doctor using a silica knife. The operation was a success, but the young king died two days later, on 6th of July 1217, due to an infection that was unpredictable for 13th century medicine. Here is kept King Enrique's skull with the terrible mark from the trepanation.

The front sepulchre is that of Prince Fernando de la Cerda, the eldest of Alfonso X (the Wise)'s sons, born to reign. His death when he was twenty-one years old (1275) prevented him from becoming king, and left the kingdom and the lawyers perplexed, as it proposed a grave problem of succession. The

23, 24 *and* **25.**
Sepulchre of Prince Alfonso de la Cerda with details of the same.

fame that could not be given to this prince by the crown was given by his sepulchre, the only one not to be violated during the invasion by the French in 1808, as it was covered by that of his son, Alfonso, now in the middle of the aisle. The body of the dead king was discovered in 1942, with its robes and apparel, which are now one of the main exhibits in the Museum of Mediaeval Cloths.

The supports and the polychrome of the tomb have deteriorated. There are castles and lions in the double row of octagons, and the rhombuses contain the stripes of Aragon. Prince Fernando inherited these coats-of-arms through his parents, King Alfonso X and Queen Violante, or Yolanda of Aragon.

The large lancet arch over the sepulchre is of interesting artistic value. It is made up of three archivolts, the central one decorated with castles and lions and the side ones with vine leaves and bunches of grapes. It looks like the doorway of a small church or, rather, the entrance to the Holy City that they wanted to paint on the background of the tympanum. On the celestial Jerusalem stands a Calvary that seems to be forced by the space in its dimensions. Jesus, as well as Mary and John, are dressed in clothes with strange folds and their proportions are wide rather than elegant. On crossed branches two angels are holding the sun and the moon. The cenotaph is crowned with the shield of Castile and León at the end of a sharp gable. All this appears to be late 13th or early 14th century work.

Prince Fernando de la Cerda (he was called this because he was born with a long bristle «cerda» on his chest) was the father of Prince Alfonso. He claimed his inheritance from his father and his right to reign. He was helped in this by his grandfather Alfonso X, but came up against opposition from his uncle, Prince Sancho, who in fact reigned as Sancho IV and was justly known as «the Brave». Unfortunately there was a civil war; Prince Alfonso was not killed then; he died in 1333.

His tomb rests on two lions which are looking at each other and is similar to that of his father in the type of motives worked on it. Mudejar knots form octagons containing castles and lions. Prince Alfonso used fleurs-de-lys because of his mother Blanche, daughter of St. Louis of France –for this reason they appear in the empty spaces. The frontispieces, which are triangular because of the shape of the lid, show Christ between the Virgin Mary and St. John on the one, and the Virgin seated with the Child in her arms together with two kneeling angels on the other. This sepulchre seems to have been made in the 14th century, although some claim it to be older.

This small sarcophagus worked in stone contains one of the small children of the royal family; you can read that it belongs to the young Princess Leonor, but it may really be that of the baby Prince Sancho, born in 1181. In either case, this small tomb is a coffer of artistic and philosophical beauty. We can see the death bed and two relatives with the body, while the soul is being carried up to heaven by two angels; on either side are arches with small towers and officials of the church. The head of the coffin also shows arches and small towers; each of the four arches contains a person in pain. The opposite end shows a laurel wreath with an Agnus Dei in the centre.

On the lid is a depiction of the soul being received by Christ. There are also two figures whose presence we cannot explain: that of St. Martin on horseback giving his cape to a poor man, and a mythological griffin. The most interesting thing, although hardly fitting for a child, is the inscription that reads, «Whoever you are you will fall into death, so take heed and weep for mine. I am what you will be and was what you are now; I beg you to pray for me. 1194. P.M.F.». The last three letters must refer to the name of the artist «Pedro Martínez made this» (Petrus Martini fecit). The date is that of the final years of Romanesque art, to which this tomb belongs.

The undecorated tomb of Prince Fernando also stands in this aisle. He died in 1211, to the bitter grief of his parents. «His death produced the lamentation of the land and the lamentation of the father, who could not be consoled because, so history tells us, he considered him and he saw in him the mirror of his life, the prince was the hope of the people»... This sepulchre must have been moved from the chapel of La Asun-

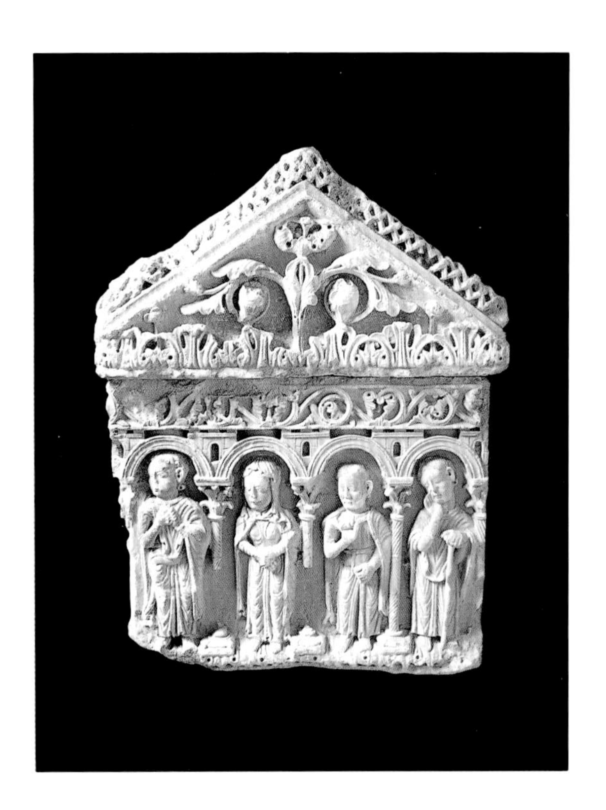

26. *Detail of the small coffin.* ▶

27. *Coffin of one of the children of Alfonso VIII.*

28. *Front of the founders' sepulchre.*

ción or the *Claustrillas,* where the upper part that protected it can be seen.

There is, finally, another sepulchre which is polemic as to whom it contains; according to this recent card it is Prince Sancho, son of St. Fernando. It was previously said to be an unknown Don Nuño, or also to be Alfonso X, the Wise. Whatever the truth may be, the box is very similar to another we saw in the chapel of San Juan Bautista, with round and trilobate aches housing sixteen identical shields on the lid and the front. Towers appear above the arches and the remaining decoration is vegetal, with a large cross decorated with volutes. This style corresponds with the date on the inscription beside the front «On Thursday the 23rd of July, 1209 (1247 A.D.), Don Nuño died in León».

V. The Founders' Sepulchres

Now we will move on to the central aisle, which is of graceful height and flooded with light. It is time to introduce ourselves to the extremely serene monarchs of Castile, Alfonso the Good and Queen Eleanor Plantagenet, or of England. Here they are, attentive to the prayers of supplication, to afflictions, joyful because their work still stands, eight hundred years after its completion. They are graceful to the Creator because their wish expressed in the foundation letter of 1187 is still being fulfilled «In Santa María la Real the Cistercian Rule will be observed *perpetually*»... «This confirmed, stable institution must remain inviolable at all

29. *The founders' sepulchre, in the central aisle.* ▶

30. *The founders' sepulchre. King Alfonso gives the founding document to Doña Misol.*

times». This is their double sepulchre, considered the heart of the convent.

The sovereigns' horizontal thrones were placed here, as has already been mentioned, in 1279. It was on the 4th of September. The church had been completed and the altars were shining at the front. Since he was in Burgos at the time, Miguel Sánchez, the Bishop of Albarracín, officiated in the blessing of the altars and the moving of the founders' coffins. The abbess, Doña María Gutiérrez and another nun, Princess Berenguela, daughter of St. Fernando, presided.

Alfonso VIII died on the 6th of October 1214, in the land of Arévalo, at the age of fifty-nine, «He fell ill of a strong fever which took such a hold of him that there he died of it... With him died the glory and nobleness of Castile»... Thus would write his great-grandson Alfonso the Wise. He continued: «Then this King Alfonso was taken to Burgos and buried in the Convent of Huelgas, the one he built near Burgos». Alfonso VIII had not had an easy life, governing Castile from fortresses and from military encampments for half a century. Roses did not deck all his paths, nor was it all conquests like in Cuenca or victories like in

Las Navas. He suffered defeats, like the terrible one in Alarcos, treason and disappointments. He enjoyed the love of his wife and children, but suffered the wounds of the death of several of them, especially that of Fernando who died in the splendour of youth, only twenty years old. He was consequent with his Christian beliefs, and he was known as «the Good». His sepulchre was placed in the *Caustrillas* and remained there for sixty-five years. A respectful veneration grew up around it and he was considered a saint. They even opened up a small door in the sepulchre (traces of it can still be seen) so that his devotees could touch the relic of his body.

Queen Eleanor could not bear being separated from Alfonso, whom she had so greatly loved for forty-four years. The solitude asphyxiated her and she died twenty-five days later, on 31st of October, aged fifty-four. The temperament of the Plantagenets flowed in her. «She was very beautiful», wrote the chronicler, and this, too, was how she was considered by the people, the courtiers and the jongleurs, whose songs and verses she loved to hear. «She was a very good queen, chaste, noble and wise, very understanding, and with the finest of manners», wrote her friend and admirer Jiménez de Rada. She was brought to the *Claustrillas,* to be beside her husband and together they sleep and wait.

Their sepulchres are privileged, facing the high altar; they are trapezoidal, with a roof-shaped lid. Four threatening lions support them. The main, most repetitive ornamentation has as a motif a castle with three merlon-shaped towers, showing a door and embrasures. The body of the double cenotaph, on the sides and on the four sloping sides of the lids, is covered with castles within trilobulate arches resting on columns showing capitals decorated with leaves. The castle fields are separated by borders also decorated with leaves.

The castle was King Alfonso's only, much loved coat-of-arms. He was king only of Castile, and he served his country and even spilt blood to expand it. The castle was his sign, seal and banner. Some historians believe that it was him who adopted as the emblem of the kingdom the golden castle, masoned in sable (black) and lightened with azure on a field of gules (red).

On the frontispiee facing the altar King Alfonso's sarcophagus again shows the castle in a more refined form, so much so that the large windows and rose windows make it look more like a palace than a fortress containing weapons. Beside it, within the field of an escutcheon are the arms of Queen Eleanor –the three crowned lions of the House of Plantagenet. On the triangles of the lid is the humanised soul of Queen Eleanor, dressed and crowned, being carried to heaven on a cloth held by two angels. On that of King Alfonso two angels delicately wave a fleur-de-lys cross, no doubt in memory of the victory at Las Navas, obtained on the Day of the Holy Cross (16th of July).

On the opposite side, at the head, is the resplendent, majestic figure of Alfonso VIII, seated on his throne, with a crown atop his long hair and a curly beard, dressed in a tunic and cloak and Moorish buskins. He is handing the foundation document to Doña Misol, the first abbess, and her companions, who are kneeling clothed in habits and wimples. The royal seal hangs from the roll of parchment. Above Queen Eleanor's lions there is a Calvary; the twisted body of Christ increases the dramatism of Mary and John. The sun and the moon appear above the arms of the Cross.

31. *The abbess's seat with the staff.*

The reign of Enrique I was too short for the work on these sepulchres to be finished during it, so it became a task for Fernando III, grandson of the founders. It is said that when in the 16th century a bishop opened the coffins the body of the king was complete and recognisable; it is added that the bishop removed a ring from one of the hands as a gift for Felipe II. This monarch did not hide his disgust and ordered the bishop to give it back to its owner. The bishop died just after carrying out this mission, when on his way back to his diocese, that of Osma, in 1593.

VI. A Ship on the Waves of History and Art

In the early days of the convent, for example in 1279, the perspective from here was completely different from the one we have nowadays. The church emerged with the smell of recent lime, shone with the geometry of pillars and was covered with ribs and moulding and magnificent capitals and candlesticks. It was the pure expression of art that St. Bernard demanded in his glorious Order of Cistercium.

The early choir did not fill the space be-

32. *The choirstalls.*

33. *Partition wall in the central nave. Interior.*

34. *The Descent from the Cross on the partition wall.*

tween the large pillars, but this did happen when Ana of the House of Austria, abbess from 1611 to 1629, commissioned these harmonious simple choirstalls with cresting showing the coats-of-arms of Castile and of the House of Austria. The abbess's stall, the first on the right, is protected by the Reverend Mother's pectoral staff. On the facing music stands lie the hymnbooks of the long, devout Cistercian psalmody; these are the expression of one part of the Order's great motto: *Ora et Labora* («Work and pray»).

The necessary liturgical separation of the community from the people has always been observed, but it is unknown when the church was divided as can be seen now. That baldachin at the front prevents us from seeing the transept and the apse, although it makes up for it with other works of beauty. The enormous, splendid Calvary which crowns it was perhaps not intended for that paricular place; however the aesthetic result is very positive.

I should now like to invite you visitors to come on a mental journey to this spacious church to attend some of the ceremonies which have taken place here in the past. In just one day we will be able to relive pages of our history and events that occupy pages in the old chronicles of Castile. These very stones, this same atmosphere, this same light were witnesses to days both happy and sad, but all marked with the grandeur and dignity which our antecedents knew how to lend to important events.

Here kings were crowned with pomp and rejoicing; here kings were buried with pomp and sadness; here men were knighted to follow the paths of honour in defence of damsels, orphans and widows. So let us evoke just some of these anniversaries.

On 30th of November 1219 King Fernando (St. Fernando) was knighted. He had just been married to Beatriz of Suabia (on the 28th) and wanted to profess loyalty to the knighthood beside the sepulchre of his much admired grandfather Alfonso VIII. The people accompanied the young monarch, and the church, in as much as construction work allowed, was suitably adorned with daises for Queen Beatriz and for the Queen Mother (Berenguela), pontificials for Bishop Mauricio of Burgos and for the assistants from other dioceses, musicians and incense. Bishop Mauricio blessed the arms, the war belt and the sword, which had been placed on the altar by the king. At the end of the mass King Fernando himself put on the belt and sheathed his sword, the very sword that straight afterwards conquered the Moors in Andújar and in 1248 opened passage in Seville.

Famous knights from Europe watched over their arms here. Perhaps the most famous was Edward, King of England, who came to Burgos in 1254, when he was still Prince, to marry Princess Leonor, the sister of Alfonso X. The event was recorded in the following way by the King of Spain: «The first time I came to Burgos after being crowned king, Prince Edward, the eldest son and heir of King Henry of England, came here and was knighted by me in the Convent of Santa María la Real, Burgos, and married my sister Princess Leonor»... This wedding and knighthood were so well known that the notaries in this part of the country dated their documents, «the year in which Prince Edward of England was knighted in Huelgas»...

The coronations which took place here were those of Alfonso XI, Enrique II, Juan I and Enrique III. The chronicler and chancellor Pedro López de Ayala describes them jubilously, in particular that of Alfonso XI and his sad and already hated wife, María of Portugal. If you one day find the peace and opportunity to do so, read the account of this ceremony in the *Crónica de Alfonso Onceno* and you will discover meticulous details about members of the nobility, the episcopacy and the high administrators of the kingdom; about the luxury displayed in sweetmeats, the trappings of the horses, clothes and other things; about the liturgy during the investiture of the knighthood and during the coronation; of the general rejoicing, which left many villages in the province of Burgos empty as the people went to take part in it. That day was followed by others, on which the king himself knighted the cream of the youth of Castile in this church. This all took place in August, 1332. So we are standing in one of the most evocative and respected places in the history of Spain.

The present feeling is less epic but more intimate, so that we can carefully examine what our eyes have ascertained as beautiful. That's right, the Calvary crowning the baldachin. It is one of the most admirable works of Gothic sculpture, and there are certainly famous pieces. The artist depicted the Descent from the Cross and therefore added to the inevitable figues of Christ, His mother and His favourite disciple those of

35, 36 *and* **37.** *Three details from the partition wall.*

38 *and* **39.**
Sepulchre
of Queen Berenguela
(13th century).

40. *Sepulchre of Blanca of Portugal.*

Nicodemus and Joseph of Arimathea. Three values should be admired in this group: the *realism* emanating from the figures, from the inertia of Christ's dead body, through the weeping of John and the serene understanding of Mary to the cares applied by Nicodemus and Joseph; the *integration* within the space given so that the anonymous artist did not encounter obstacles, and the scenic *mobility* of the characters, who still breathe the breath of their creator. It is late 13th century.

The wooden baldachin is divided into three parts; the two Renaissance right feet stand on stone bases which support an elegant gilded cornice. Until recently the Sacrament was kept in the left-hand section in a beautiful sacrarium which was thought to be the casket in which Miramamolin kept the Koran, taken from him in the Battle of Las Navas. There is a varied assortment of relics, but the best piece of work here is the relief of The Last Supper, attributed to Diego de Siloé because of the expression and detail of its figures. The wall which forms a corner with the baldachin is decorated with reliefs of the Passion and the childhood of Christ. The middle section of the baldachin, which must have been completed in about 1520, shows beautifully painted double leaves and representations of Mary and St. Peter and St. Paul. The section on the right is dominated by a beautiful figure of Santa María la Real, surrounded by the apostles Philip and John and by relics. On the side there are more scenes of the infancy of Christ in bas-relief.

On the walls are hangings with pictures of Roman emperors and above the starting point of the choir is a very fine organ which is used to accompany the psalmody of the nuns. Here it should be noted that from the

41. *Interlocking of castles and lions on the sepulchre of Queen Blanca of Portugal.*

42. *Picture of a Roman emperor on a wall hanging.*

first mediaeval days of the convent music has always been one of its artistic pursuits.

Funeral art is in evidence in various ways in this aisle. This coffin in worked stone is the sepulchre of Princess Berenguela, daughter of the king St. Fernando, who was a nun in this convent from 1242 to 1288, the probable year of her death. This sepulchre had not been made for her, but for her grandmother, Berenguela the Great, but the will the gradmother had made forbidding any kind of decoration on her coffin had greater power than the admiration felt for her.

The trapezoidal sepulchre is placed on two lions looking at each other, with towers behind their heads. The most interesting feature of this coffin is the high-reliefs depicting scenes from the infancy of Christ. The front shows six low trefoil arches with gables. Between the gables are towers with battlements. The arches are unsupported, except in the centre, where Joseph seems to be holding them up.

A page drives his donkey laden with presents for the Three Wise Men to offer to the Child, who is sitting on His mother's knee; Joseph, with a stick in his hand, watches the scene. Next, Herod hands an officer the order to kill the Innocent, which is carried out in a brutal way. The slope of the lid inclined towards this side shows six pictures of the infancy of Christ, beginning with the Annunciation and finalising with the Flight to Egypt; the arches are supported by small columns with bases and capitals. The other slope shows castles, lions and German eagles of the Suabia family. The front shows the Coronation of Our Lady by God the Father, both seated; two angels hold processional candles, and on the upper section two more angels move incense burners. The side with the feet shows, within an arch with a gable, the very typical scene of the carrying of the soul from the deathbed to heaven. Here, a bishop and an abbot are present at the death.

The name of the craftsman who made this interesting late 13th century sarcophagus is unknown. Also unknown is the one who made the sepulchre opposite, somewhat later, according to historians. Here lies Princess Blanca, born in 1259, daughter of King Sancho III of Portugal, and grandaughter of Alfonso X of Spain. She was young when she came to Spain and she seems to have been involved in some kind of flirtation the fruit of which was the Grand Master of the Order of Calatrava. She entered the convent at the age of thirty-six and she became «the column, firmament and protector of the convent and of the needy». She must have been interested in the humanities, for she had the Hebrew book *The Battles of God* translated into Spanish. She died in 1321.

Her trapezoidal coffin is supported by two lions. A lovely design of eight-pointed stars entwined with such grace that it seems Mudejar covers the box and its lid. In the middle of the stars are the castles and lions of the monarchs of Spain and the coat-of-arms of Portugal.

We cannot leave this place without showing some admiration to one of the most excellent women in the history of Spain, to Queen Berenguela, daughter of the founders and mother of Fernando III (St. Fernando). There she lies in that plain, cold coffin, she who was twice queen, greatly loved by her people, whom she served bounteously and intelligently. Using political mastery and shedding no blood she brought about the definitive union of the kingdoms of Castile and León. She died in 1246 after having rendered transcendental service to Spain. Honour and glory to her.

43. *Sepulchre of Queen Berenguela the Great.*

VII. The chapel of San Juan

The nuns did not wish to leave the separation wall between their inner recess and the part of the church for the public plain, so they decorated it with different pieces from altars which had been removed from elsewhere for a variety of reasons. The nuns' own confession box was also decorated.

Of great interest is the central Crucifixion scene since the figure of Christ appears with only castles decorating his loin cloth, which would imply a date before that of 1230, the year when the kingdoms of Castile and León were united. However, the figures of Mary and St. John appear to be successively later. On the left, between elements of Corinthian architecture, is St. John the Evangelist, with St. Marina being burnt at the stake and other small statues. On the right there is another series of small statues, reliefs of St. Anne, St. Peter, St. Paul and St. Michael, and a representation of the Virgin Mary.

The series of sepulchres continues in the aisle, some with unfinished decoration. Of interest is the coffin containing the body of María de Almenar, who died, according to the epitaph on the lid, in 1234, which corresponds to 1196 A.D. María de Almenar is an almost unknown lady, but it is suspected that she was in very close contact with the royal family and that she may have been nanny to Princess Blanca, the future mother of St. Louis, King of France.

We can read here that this sepulchre holds the body of Queen Leonor who was Queen of León; her nephew Pedro I had her killed. This act was carried out in the

44. *Crucifixion scene in the chapel of San Juan.*

45. *Wing of the cloisters of San Fernando.*

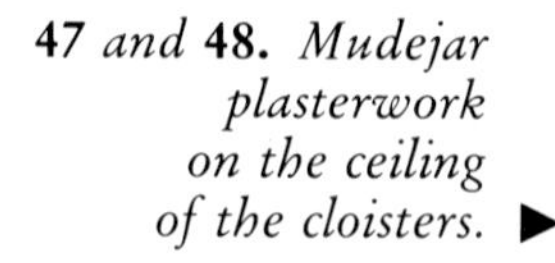

47 *and* **48.** *Mudejar plasterwork on the ceiling of the cloisters.* ▶

46. *Door from the church to the cloisters of San Fernando.*

Castle of Castrojeriz by Moorish executioners as no Christian wanted to put his hands on the annointed lady. In Castrojeriz it is believed that the body of the unfortunate queen, killed in 1359, is conserved in the collegiate church of the town.

Only the lid is illustrated with figures of men, animals and plants, very typical of the Romanesque style popular at that time. On the front slope, in a series of round arches, is the very frequent representation of death and the carrying of the soul to heaven. In one part are four bishops in pontificial clothes and in the other seven lay people. The slope towards the wall is decorated with foliaged volutes, as is one of the two borders right around the lid; the other slope shows some dogs that are chasing harpies and dragons.

VIII. The Cloisters of San Fernando

We leave the church through a Gothic door decorated with foliage and castles; the leaves are a fine example of the Mudejar woodwork that can be seen in this convent. These spacious cloisters were completed in the reign of St. Fernando, who had close ties with this convent in which his mother and his maternal grandparents lie to rest.

The aspect of this wide enclosure and its four aisles of 45 m. each must have been very different from that of today. Then it would have been a space open to the air and sun through its lancet arches and the columns that supported it. But cloisters, which are such a beautiful sight on which to feast the eyes, usually present one great inconvinience to those who live in monasteries and

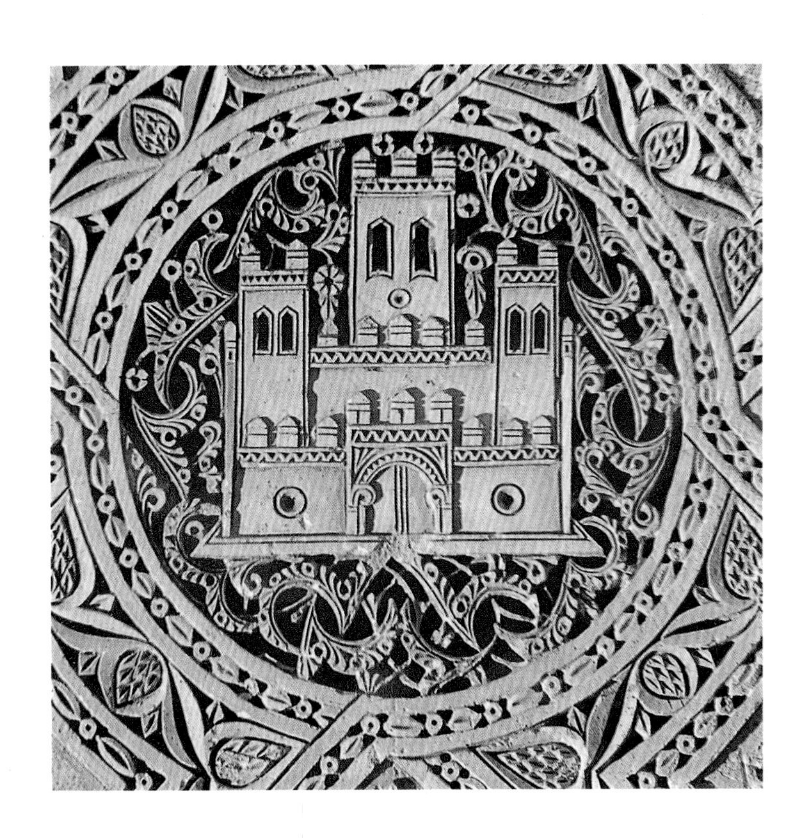

49. *Door of the sacristy.*

convents permanently: the cold they bring.

It should not be forgotten that we are on the high flat lands of Burgos, where the winters are generally severe. Every day the Cistercian nuns have to cross here on their way to the choir, refectory, chapter room and divine office. This fact brought about substantial changes: all the columnade was replaced by a wall with some windows and the doors leading to the flagstoned courtyard in which a fountain in the shape of a goblet within a circular trough plays. Also, to support the upper galleries, pilasters with segmental arches like railings were built.

The first great surprise these cloisters have to offer us are the pointed barrel vaults with transverse arches that divide them. These vaults show very interesting plasterwork decorations in Mudejar style, realised between 1230 and 1260. It is a shame that the modifications and work carried out in the cloisters have greatly damaged these decorations and early blue, ochre and black paintwork. The vestiges that remain are enough for us to be able to guess at how amazing the ceiling of these cloisters must have been in the middle of the 13th century. Academics consider that the variety and richness of this plasterwork made it «the first of all the Hispanic-Arab examples known, including the best in the Alhambra».

The visitor must be wondering: «But, why the artistic presence, in these and other details seen, of a race and a religion so different from the owners of Huelgas and the mediaeval period?». The answer is both easy and necessary: the Middle Ages were very long and contained a little of everything, but the visitor should also think about the continuous, violent intolerance between Christians and Muslims, between Spaniards and Arabs in mediaeval times. There were happy moments of understanding and collaboration between Moors, Jews and Christians and there was a synthesis between them and their beliefs. In art, there were Mudejar and Mozarabic craftsmen.

As it was founded by royalty and was a royal pantheon, as it had strict relations with the monarchs and their closest relatives, as it enjoyed privileges and economic possibilities, Santa María la Real could approach the Mudejar world and receive from it very valuable examples of its art. That world was not far away: Al'Andalus was also showing signs of life in Burgos where a community of Moors

50. *Detail of the door of the sacristy.*

who were highly appreciated for their craftsmanship were living peacefully.

Mudejars worked in this convent from the very moment of its foundation. King Fernando IV regulated this participation in 1304 by exempting twelve Moors who worked on the convent as officials from paying tributes. In 1367 Felipe II increased this exemption to all the Moors working on the construction of Huelgas.

Because of this royal dispensation the Mudejars worked very hard here and left their elegant seal on this convent. The decorations on the vaults of the cloisters of San Fernando are very varied and are true to the style and taste of Arabic art, which are, as is well known, based on foliage worked on plaster, geometric patterns of which the knots are the most impressive, and the Mozarabic work and the epigraphs. So there are Arabic-style lines which entwine fancifully, leaves and shoots, Cufic writing and peacocks, castles, griffins and other fantastic animals. Here we can contemplate some divine art in the small part of multicoloured plasterwork that time has spared.

And here too is another admirable piece of Mudejar art–that door giving to the sacristy.

51. *Entrance to the chapter room.*

The stone section is Romanesque with double archivolts, adorned with vine and palm leaves; castles can also be seen. The leaves are in pine with walnut and boxwood panels that are so finely decorated that they seem to be made of ivory rather than of wood. The geometric patterns and the plaster-work are also magnificent, and a Cufic inscription expresses the desire for a «perfect blessing» to fall on you as you walk through this door.

There are also some chapels off the cloisters for the nuns' divine offices and for the carrying out of certain liturgical ceremonies that make use of these altars during processions. As we go round we shall also be able to see marks made by the early masons on the ashlar blocks.

IX. The Chapter Room

In all monasteries and convents the chapter room is, after the church, the most venerable and most venerated place. Here is the abbot's, or in this case the abbess's chair. In the chapter room the monks or nuns who have the right to do so deal with all the important matters concerning the observance of the Rule, their religious customs and the material business that may arise; secret votes are held for elections, including that of the abbess, and the edifying accusations of one's own defects is heard.

This canonical importance, mentioned in the old reference «the community gathered in the chapter room at the ringing of the

52. *Chapter room.* ▶

53. *Vaults in the chapter room.*

bell», is inevitably reflected in the appearance of the room itself. The architecture gives it amplitude and elegance; it is decorated with figures and other pieces of sculpture. The room also shows elements which are always of the kind accepted by the Order. So magnificent chapter rooms can be seen all over the world. The Cistercian Order is no exception, and neither is Santa María la Real, in Burgos.

Indeed, it has been said that this is the most elegant chapter room in all the Spanish Cistercian buildings. You enter it through a wide round arch supported by strong pilasters surrounded by columns both outside and in. On each side two lancet arches contain twin arches and a circular window to give light. The capitals are unworked; as this cannot be attributed to lack of funds, we must suppose that it is due to the maxim of «sobriety with elegance» imposed by St. Bernard. A saw-shaped archivolt runs around the arch on both sides: this may indicate the severity and rigour with which the dignity of the room which we are entering and the secret of what is dealt with there should be defended.

The room is composed of a square of 17 m. on each side; it is 8.60 m high. It is made up of nine sections covered with fine cross ribs coming from and going to four cylindrical pillars each surrounded by eight columns in one piece, which are 5 m. high with a diameter of 0.14 m. This surprising fineness gives them a special grace and even an appreciable harmony. At the front, on the east side, three stained-glass windows allow the light to enter. The capitals of the pillars still await a craftsman worthy of decorating them.

The walls of this highly meritorious room have been adorned with certain objects that give it a special value; pennants which flew in the victorious sky at Lepanto, brought here by the daughter of King Juan, of the House of Austria, paintings like that of the Virgin Mary protecting the Catholic Monarchs, their children and Cardinal Mendoza with her cape, tapestries and hangings with a coat-of-arms. At the front, adding excellence to the abbatical dias, in paintings attributed to Andrés López, are Felipe III and Felipe IV with their respective wives, Margarita and Mariana Ana. Also there, because she was both a member of the royal family and abbess is Princess Ana of the House of Austria, daughter of the conqueror at Lepanto, first cousin of Felipe III. She is wearing the habit of a Cistercian nun. We shall discuss her later. At each side hang original tapestries with scenes showing Marcus Aurelius and Cleopatra.

We should now pay attention to the pennant called «Pendón de las Navas de Tolosa», claimed at this battle by Alfonso VIII from Miramamolin, as he is called by Spanish chroniclers. This pennant has passed from being an expression of art to being the symbol of the final victory of the Cross over the Koran. Every year, in the moving festival of Curpillos (the day after Corpus Christi), the Captain General of Burgos waves it before the monstrance containing the sacrament, as the only invincible reality.

54. *Portrait of Princess Ana, House of Austria.*

It was a utilitarian item rather than an epic one, as it is considered to have been a part of the magnificent tent used by the Almohade sultan at the above-mantioned Battle of Las Navas de Tolosa. Its artistic and mythical value was not reduced by the fact that it was donated to this convent by King St. Fernando later, after its being carried in some of his successful campaigns in the south.

55. *Flemish tryptych of the Descent from the Cross.*

This exceptional tapestry, measuring 3.30 by 2.20 m., is woven in silver thread and coloured silk, and is the finest existing example of Almohade art. The brightness of the colours and the perfection and fantasy of the designs really draw one's attention. A small eight-pointed star acts as the focal point of this object of beauty and is the axis of two other increasingly larger ones placed within a crown of circles and stars.

Four stars, each with a blue nucleus, mark the corners of a square containing the central part; the remaining space in the corners has been finely decorated and in the narrow part between the two lower stars we can see the only animal figure on the pennant: three lions rampant. The four sides show the following Cufic inscriptions of texts from the Koran:

Along the top: «Oh believer! I shall show thee a use of money that will free thee from the torments of hell»...

Along the bottom: «I shall introduce thee into garadens irrigated by flowing water, into the enchanted rooms of the Gardens of Eden»...

To our right: «This will be more useful to thee if thou understandeth it. God will pardon thee thy trepasses»...

To our left: «Believe in God and in His messenger, fight on the path of God, sacrifice thy goods and thy person»...

The upper part is composed of three sections. Two are the same; in them are ten rectangles showing the Islamic confession of faith «Only Allah is God and Mohammed is his prophet». Between these two sections is the other, which is twice as big and shows the following inscription. «I seek refuge in God as I flee from Satan, the stoned one. In the name of God, the clement and merciful one, may the blessing of Allah be upon Mohammed and his followers». There are more words; in the very centre of the tapestry the word «Empire» is repeated and in each of the eight lower circles the miraculous hands of the artists have written: «The eternal empire, perpetual happiness»; «Perpetual salvation»; «Praise be to God for His gifts»; «Eternal health».

This is the best example of the art brought to Spain by these people who came from Islamic darkest Africa but later disappeared from the scenes of history after their definitive downfall in this country.

X. The Modern Museum

In the year of the Eight Hundredth Anniversary of the Founding of the Convent a museum was installed in the following room with interesting 16th to 20th century pieces. It is believed that in the early days of the convent this was the entrance hall, and the door, now a large window, seems to prove it. The fact that it was used for something in particular can be seen from the plasterwork on the ceiling and on the frieze.

Along the centre of the ceiling runs an ornamental frieze worked by extremely deft hands, showing Castilian castles, plasterwork and inscriptions in Arabic. At the end, the castles at either side of the window show which kingdom this convent belonged to. The side fascia is unusual with its long Latin text from the Psalms and the very important detail of the date of the termination of the work: «The year Mil CCCXIII» (that is, 1275 A.D.).

56. *Hall with showcases in the Modern Museum.*

More recent exhibits by various artists can be seen in the showcases in this museum. The first piece is a 16th century chalice in silver plated with gold, which is followed by other fine pieces, generally of a liturgical nature, such as chalices, crosses, rosaries, reliquaries, a Calvary, a reliquary in gilded bronze, cruets, ciboriums, monstrances, candelabra and pendants and earrings which may have been offered by devout ladies to statues of Our Lady.

On the other side are surgical instruments from the Hospital del Rey which used to belong to this convent, but is now part of the National Heritage. They are significant for the history of medicine and to understand part of the suffering of the human race. There are also porcelain utensils, pots and jars from old pharmacies and wide bowls with the anagram of Christ (J.H.S). This was a compulsory sign on all the convent crockery and gave rise to the saying: «Until I see you, my Lord!» from those who eagerly emptied their cup of wine or bowl of soup.

57. *Detail of the «Claustrillas».*

XI. The «Claustrillas»

Now we shall leave the cloisters of San Fernando by the doorway giving to the Romanesque cloisters and the passageway leading to the chapel of Santiago. Like the previous part of the convent, this is decorated with Mudejar plasterwork; an ornamental frieze, a sort of carpet decorated with castles and rosettes with knots is fixed on the ceiling, and runs right along the centre of it. At the top of the walls an equally beautiful large border in the same style includes, in Latin, the «Salve» to Our Lady and a prayer for sunset from the *Book of Hours* which, translated, means: «We beseech thee to visit this house and to banish from here any ambush by the enemy». These are also 13th century pieces of work. Some noble coats-of-arms belonging to abbesses from the 19th century hang on the walls.

This is a delightful corner, an oasis of tranquility, colour and music. Here history and art intertwine with legends and harmony while the small fountain issues verses which the birds weave into poems. These cloisters are probably the oldest part of the convent; they may even have existed before the foundation of the Cistercian Convent as the central part of a mansion the monarchs had here to which they came to rest and enjoy themselves. The style is late Romanesque.

Each of the four galleries contains twelve round arches supported by twin columns showing wide capitals and undecorated abaci. In the middle of each gallery is a pillar with sackcloth on the lower part, between the columns of the following arches. The arcades, which are undecorated, are of sober appearance.

The influence of Santo Domingo de Silos can be appreciated in the decoration of these cloisters, particularly in the foliage –nearly always leaves and shoots in varied patterns. The pillar in the north wing offers a curious urban scene: that of a 12th century city, with walls and battlements, with horseshoe arches, churches and other buildings. Is it a representation of the city of Burgos during the reign of Alfonso VIII?

The age of these cloisters, the composure of their lines, the sunny surroundings and the intimacy here transport us to the early years of the foundation of the convent of Santa María la Real. The voices and images of those times are still strong we can hear Queen Eleanor chatting to Doña Misol and her nuns while their hands are hard at work making things for the altar. In the other wing King Alfonso is walking with his second lieutenant and steward and some prelate speaking seriously, in low voices, about state affairs.

58. *The «Claustrillas».* ▶

59 *and* **60.**
The chapel of La Asunción.
Doorway and detail.

61. *Painted figure of the Virgin with Child.*

XII. The Chapel of La Asunción

Within the apparent humility of this chapel beats the very heart in both architecture and decoration of the Almohade art still to be found in Spain. It appears to have undergone some changes, but its singularity is obvious. The walls are made of brick and it measures little over 6 m^2. However, it is completely true to Almohade architecture and sobriety, and it is curious how, during the 13th century, two such completely different yet similar tendencies, as are those of St. Bernard and of Africa, should meet up together in Huelgas.

Just within the doorway are three small, lovely vaults with white loop-shaped ornaments: it is a sky of stalagmites, loops and fine shoots. What could be considered the presbytery shows a sealed up door in the north wall. In the east wall there are two tiny niches with horseshoe arches and seven other small arches in the archivolt. There are two others similar to these, although bigger, in the south wall. From the corners of the presbytery, almost at floor level, rise four squinch arches which convert the square into an octagonal shape. Two large windows with unusual plasterwork standing between other blocked arches give light to the chapel. The vault is an eight-pointed star, formed by the crossing of four pairs of plain parallel arches. An altar was recently placed under this exclusive piece of work and on it a beautiful painted stone image of the Virgin with Child; while He plays with His mother's hair she offers Him a gift.

Through the two arches in the south wall is a small room with wooden pillars showing Arabic designs and inscriptions. On the other side of the arches is something as unexpected and paradoxical in this place as the above-mentioned Virgin: a Christian, Romanesque sepulchral arch which stood over the tomb of Prince Fernando, who died in 1211 and was greatly mourned by all as he was brought to this chapel. The coffin was moved to the chapel of Santa Catalina, where it still stands.

This surprising sepulchral arch is a masterpiece of geometry and is made up of various elements: two identical round arches with circlets decorated with small pyramids, each with four foils; the arches support a pendant or hanging arch. A large arch runs around both; it is depressed and undecorated. In the remaining spaces there is a scene of the carrying of the soul to paradise, and on the right and the left two harpies. Ogees decorated with rosettes support the whole; they are resting on columns with capitals decorated with foliage. This work dates from the early 13th century.

XIII. The Chapel of Santiago

Before entering this chapel we sould admire the strong fabrication of the east arm of the transept and the head of the convent church. The door to the chapel is a somewhat pointed horseshoe arch resting on two marble columns and Arabic capitals which point to Andalusian origins.

62. *Entrance to the chapel of Santiago.*

The chapel is divided into two parts. The first has altars in different styles along the walls and on the floor some tombs with stones showing coats-of-arms. The passage to the following part –the presbytery, which no longer contains its former altar and baldachin– is through a beautiful arch in the same style as the former. On the spandrels opposite you there are two wooden figures, not originally in this chapel.

The presbytery is quadrangular, so you can admire the decoration of the inside of the arch, with plasterwork and shells which may owe their inspiration to the proximity of St. Jack's Way. There is also a frieze around the other three walls, similar to those we have already seen in the museum and the portico.

63. *The chapel of Santiago.*

64. *Jointed Gothic figure of Santiago*

Casatilian castles emerge from among eight-sided knots and from shoots and spirals. The similarity to other parts of the convent indicates that this chapel must have been built before 1275. The ceiling is of wood; its hips give it the form of a trough. Decorated with stars and painted, it shows a central panel. It is thought to have been painted with enamel originally.

This beautiful corner also has its own evocations deried from the figure at the front of the chapel. It is the apostle St. James, to whom the tiny church is dedicated. It is a wooden figure which was made and painted in the 13th century. The right arm is jointed and in its hand it is holding a sword which was originally made of steel but is now made of wood.

This figure reminds us of God's great knight, the recruiter of knights errants, not only of the pilgrim who is suggested by the scallop shells opposite. Tradition confirms that here the rite of being knighted was carried out, and that having spent the night watching over his arms and having heard mas at dawn, generally officiated by the bishop, the novice was tapped on the shoulder by the apostle himself. The figure may have been taken to the main aisle of the church on very important occasions to give more pomp to the liturgy. It was a source of pride to go out to the battlefield and onto the road to adventures armed as a knight in Santa María la Real in Burgos, and by the arm of the apostle himself, the patron saint of all worthy, clean souls.

XIV. The Museum of Mediaeval Cloths

A group of old and unusual buildings like these that we are visiting demands a great deal of attention from the National Heritage. Some are unique expressions of certain cultures, works of art which are not only rare

65. *Frieze and coffered ceiling in the chapel of Santiago.*

but also dangerously delicate. This is the case of the mediaeval cloths which, having been removed from the coffins already seen, are exhibited in the Modern Museum in special cases with particular methods of conservation.

The National Heritage experts discovered a scientifically ideal place for the installation of the Museum of Mediaeval Cloths in the unused granary of the convent, situated beside the south wing of the cloisters of San Fernando and separated from it by the recently discovered corridor of the Conversas (nuns mainly dedicated to craftwork).

The granary, as its name suggests, was the store room and pantry for the convent food. Above it was the barn or tithe house where the cereals brought in payment by the convent tenants were kept. Not all the granary has been restored in the recent building work, just the central part, and all the showcases containing the cloths have been placed below its double bays. The result is a very fine room with three Cistercian ogival arches. In the north wall we can see three chutes down which the grain was poured from the barn. A great deal of attention has been paid to the problems of damp and temperature, so that the exhibits are not affected by them. The showcases have the same form as the sepulchres and in some cases are even of the same size.

The peace of the dead has repeatedly been disturbed in Huelgas. Sometimes for canonical and legitimate reasons, others because of looting, as happened with the outer sepulchres in the Caballeros cloisters, and when the invadors passed through in 1808. This plundering has caused irreparable damage and at times it was not only great but also badly used by the plunderers. In 1942 the National Heritage created a commission of experts who carried out some

66. *The Museum of Mediaeval Cloths, in the former granary of the convent.*

admirable research and recognition work. The pieces collected as a result of this were used to begin what was first known as the Museum of Fine Cloths, which has been reorganised into the museum we are now visiting; it constitutes the finest of its kind, because of the value, originality and uniqueness of its elements. It was opened by H.M. the King and H.M. the Queen of Spain, the noble patrons of the convent, on the 1st. of June, 1987.

These cloths, which have been repaired with great love and technique show us how the upper classes of Castile dressed at the height of the Middles Ages, and explain the subtle commercial and industrial relations that existed between the Christian and Arab members of society. There are complete trousseaus which lead to a better understanding of the cloths on the statues in the cathedrals and those in the miniatures in the codices. Such are those obtained from the sepulchres of Prince Fernando de la Cerda and Leonor of Castile, daughter of the founders and Queen of Aragon.

We shall pay more attention to these two exhibits, although many other cloths and garments also merit close attention, such as these belonging to Prince Fernando (d. 1311), in silk and thread braided with gold –made with the Moorish tapestry technique, Almohade style. It is decorated with geometric designs and wording. One sentence reads, «The Lord is the renewer of consolation».

Prince Fernando de La Cerda's coffin appeared intact, covered with an outer lining of a beautiful piece of brocade measuring over 6 m^2, made of silk and threads braided with gold. Circles and hexagonal medallions contain face-to-face lions and turkeys beside the tree of life in shades of gold,

67. *Long fur-lined robe belonging to Prince Fernando de la Cerda, Museum of Mediaeval Cloths.*

68. *Biretta made of taffeta, gold and seed pearls belonging to Prince Fernando de la Cerda.*

69. *Material that lined one of the coffins in the royal pantheon.*

ochre and purple. In the middle are a silver cross and the arms of the crown, which Prince Fernando never even girded. The inner lining is of taffeta worked with silk and gold thread and decorated with braids of various colours worked with the words, «Praise be to God» and ears of wheat and stars. The box and lid, made of resinous wood, are also lined on the outside with taffeta decorated with face-to-face griffins and geometrical patterns.

From one large piece of silk brocade with threads braided with gold and gilded silver three garments (a cloak, a long fur-lined robe and a jubbah) were made for the body of Prince Fernando. They are decorated with the coats-of-arms of Castile and León, as was the fashion then in the north of Spain where they favoured heraldic designs. The cloak is wide and still has the tapes to secure it. The robe still conserves the fur with which it was originally lined –this kind of garment was used by men and women alike. The jubbah was a Moorish garment with narrow sleeves and an opening on the left-hand side, which was also very popular among Christians. This particular one is lined with crimson taffeta.

But as well as these garments the coffin also contained other material signs of the very high social importance of its owner. These are his biretta, ring, sword and baldric. The biretta still shines as it did on great occasions at court. It is made of white canvas, lined with crimson taffeta, and decorated on the outside with castles and lions. The castles are in fine silver on a field of coral, with blue beads for the doors and windows. The red, embroidered lions are rampant, on a field of white seed pearls. At the top and bottom are gold borders, decorated with the quartered royal coat-of-arms, with sapphires and garnet stones between. It is obviously Castilian.

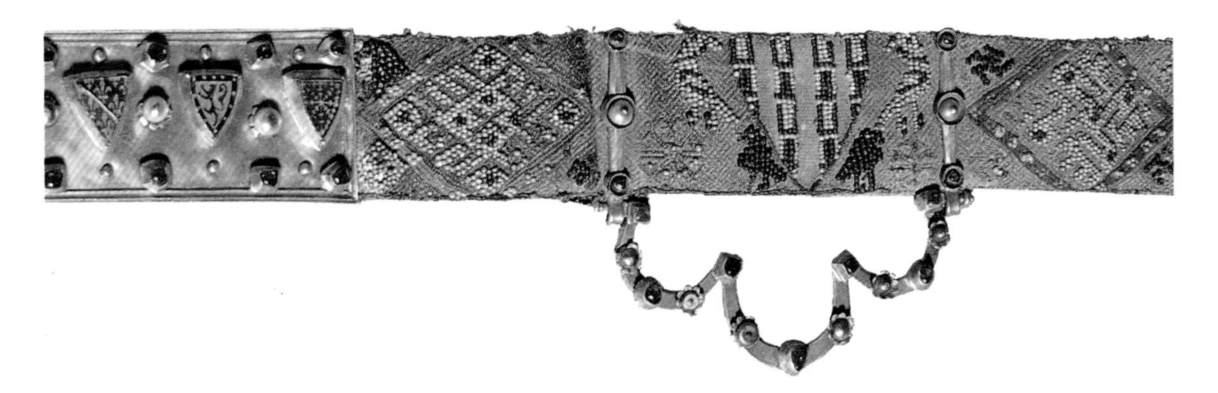

70. *Baldric belonging to Prince Fernando.*

On the other hand, the belt is a piece of work from overseas, as can be seen from the heraldry decorating it –ten coats-of-arms, all apparently belonging to British lineages. How did the Prince of Castile manage to have this? It is 192 cm long and therefore reaches the ground; the buckle is of gilded silver, as is the tribolate part in which to hang the sword; it is decorated with sapphires, pearls and cornelians. The sword is of an extremely military simplicity. On the ring finger of his right hand, which was placed on the pommel of the sword hilt, was a gold ring set with a garnet stone en-

71. *Long fur-lined robe found in one of the sepulchres.*

72. *Las Navas Cross.*

circled by eight small beryls. The spurs are Moorish in style and show extremely fine workmanship; they are made of iron, with silver plating and Moorish decorations. The small attachment chains are made of silver, with buckles and chapes decorated with eight-pointed stars, castles and lions. The skill of the craftsman who produced these fine examples of metalwork is amazing.

Leonor of Castile, the first wife of Jaime I of Aragon, whose marriage was annulled because of close kinship in 1229, retired to Burgos with her sister Bereguela, who was also separated from her husband. Some interesting items were found in her sepulchre, such as the pillow, which is made of two different pieces of material, one being silk taffeta and the other silk brocade. The first has an Almohade-style tapestry border, the inscriptions on which read «Good luck and happiness». The second is in bright colours and shows various designs. Also on show is Leonor's tunic: it has no sleeves, and a tape does up the opening on one of the sides. The brocade of which it is made is of high quality. These were fashionable in Spain until the 16th century. The fur-lined robe, with similar decorations to the tunic, is blue and green.

In two showcases you can see the material which lined the tomb and the pillow of María de Almenar. The lining is a large piece of material, 2.25 m. long, which is bright crimson. The middle is decorated with circles showing Cufic inscriptions inside which pairs of lions turning to face each other watch over the tree of life, which is very simple in design. These figures, in accordance with the Sassanian philosophy and art to which they obviously belong, represent eternity. The material of which

73. *Detail of the pillowcase found in Berenguela the Great's coffin.*

the pillow is made is silk brocade with threads braided with gold.

From Berenguela the Great's tomb we have not only interesting, beautiful pieces of her clothing, but also the exceptional coffin pillow. It is made of silk taffeta, silk tapestry and gold thread. It is crimson in colour. In the central field, surrounded by two borders and with stars in the four corners is a circle at the top of which is written, in Arabic italics: «There is no other God than Allah». Within the said circle and on either side of what appears to be a conceptual tree of life, a young woman with almond-shaped eyes and black hair held back with a gold band plays an instrument to the sound of which a dancer performs. This is an example of Coptic art.

The sepulchre of the founding monarchs and that of their son Enrique I have proportioned less items. The various examinations carried out and the attempts to have Alfonso VIII declared a saint may have provoked spiritual covetousness and a desire on the part of the people for relics. Here is exhibited a piece of the king's cloak, of silk decorated with gold castles on a red field. The sepulchral lids of Queen Eleanor and her youngest son can also be seen.

This museum contains other cloths of equal or lesser interest, which visitors are free to admire. We shall end our tour with meritous exhibits, this cross known as Las Navas Cross since it is said to have gone into the battle with King Alfonso, and the leather case for his monstrance. The Cross is made of gilded iron and silver and is tipped with fleurs-de-lys. It is decorated with oak leaves and set with pearls and semi-precious stones. The case shows excellent repoussé work with lions, birds and plants. It is a fine example of the industrial and artistic treat-

74. *Choir of the former servants.*

75. *Tomb of Princess Ana, House of Austria.*

ment of leather in Córdoba when the city was under Arab rule.

XV. Princess Ana, House of Austria

Leaving the cloisters of San Fernando we shall enter the church through the chapel of San Juan Evangelista. It contains various styles of paintings, the most interesting being a Flemish panel depicting Joseph and Mary looking for an inn on Christmas Eve. Behind the grille is a small choir formerly used by the servants of the religious community. Our Lady of the Rosary watches over it.

We did not see everything in the main aisle when we looked at it before. Now we can admire the enormous grille in gilded wood which closes off the large nuns' choir on the west. It is in classic style with ribbed columns and a frieze topped with crests dominated by three medallions of great heraldic pomp. These show the faces of Queen Eleanor, from England, of Alfonso VIII and of Berenguela, all facing the apse of the church. Facing the east and looking very life-like are Felipe II, Carlos I and Juan, House of Austria.

The entire wall at the end of the aisle is covered by a wide, splendid altar below a dome on which shine the painted coats-of-arms of the House of Austria. The altarpiece is made up of five vertical sections and contains figures of the Virgin Mary, St. Benedict and St. Bernard. The outer sections contain a collection of small figures some of which are admirable, such as the first on our right. In the central section we can see eight paintings and other figures, as well as reliquaries. It is said that they came from the monastery of San Pedro de Carde-

76. *Painted wooden grille commissioned by Princess Ana, House of Austria.*

ña when it was abandoned in 1835. On the side walls are plain wooden choirstalls, used by the nuns who do craftwork.

Everything seen here was commissioned by Princess Ana, House of Austria, an illegitimate daughter of Juan, House of Austria, the fruit, it would seem, of a love affair of his in Italy. The child was educated in a convent and became prioress of an Augustinian convent in Madrigal de las Altas Torres. The situation in the convent in Santa María de Huelgas was not very calm at the beginning of the 17th century and there was talk of different opinions among the nuns here as to the duration of the abbess's term of office. In other to regain peace a group of Cistercians asked King Felipe II to arrange to have his cousin Ana, House of Austria, sent to Burgos as abbess for life.

Thus, with the necessary dispensations Ana changed order and convent and became the lifelong abbess of this royal convent in 1611. She proved to be an excellent administrator and a just governess. It appears that she was respected by everybody and loved by her subjects. She came here as a mature woman of forty-two and left material proof of her good works and of her pious soul. She held her post for eighteen years and then on 16th of June, 1629, she stopped.

77. A Flemish panel depicting Joseph and Mary looking for an inn in Bethlehem.

78. *Crucifixion scene in the chapel of El Salador.*

79. *Entrance to the chapel of El Salvador.*

80 *and* **81.** *The convent of Las Huelgas possesses an important collection of documents containing many manuscripts, codices and miniatures.*

Why did she stop? Did she die? For years there was a catafalque in this choir in which there was an empty coffin; on the coffin is this strange inscription: «Here lies the Excellent Lady Ana, of the House of Austria, who was the very worthy and blessed lifelong abbess of this royal convent. Died on 28th of November of M.D.C.XXLX». The way in which the date is written is also surprising. Is it 1640? Princess Ana's mysterious end has given rise to diverse interpretations, the most probable being the voluntary retirement of a sexagenarian abbess after a life laden with renown and responsibility, such as having to return interior calm and material security to Santa María de Huelgas. On the simple stone, among tiles from Talavera, we can read a name that deserves all our respect.

We leave the inner recess of the convent through the chapel of Santa Catalina, with bright altars at the front and the back. Some of the paintings are worthy of attention –they are from differente periods and it is not always easy to identify the artist.

XVI. Travellers, it is time to move on...

The flame of Santa María la Real de Huelgas, in Burgos, is still bright in our eyes.

82. *The way to the choir.*

83. *«Ora et labora».*

You travellers have stepped before the art and history produced, received and kept in this unique convent, which is over eight hundred years old. However, it should be remembered that what you have visited is only part of Santa María. There are other aspects which cannot be seen and retain their secret.

There are, for example, very fine archives in the convent which allow for a rigorous, detailed reconstruction of what has happened from 1187 until today. Many fine things have been written about this convent. Another aspect is the constant appreciation of music on the part of the Cistercian community. This is one of the most stimulating subjects for specialists who see this as one of the most luminous centres of European music in the Middle Ages. The high level of culture can be seen in other, minority arts such as the miniatures in codices, beautiful pages of which were produced here.

There is yet another famous building, that of the Hospital del Rey, also founded by Alfonso VIII and Queen Eleanor. It was one of the most important institutions on St. Jack's Way, and subject to the authority of the abbess of Santa María. Throughout Europe people had heard of the quality and generosity of this hospital in which all the pilgrims on their way to Santiago de Compostela received assitance and lodging. Times have passed and the function of the hospital has changed, but the figure of the pilgrim mother feeding her baby which Diego de Siloé formed on the doors of the hospital church serves as a golden symbol of the preoccupation and the devotion of this Cistercian convent to its work of charity –the Hospital del Rey.

The conservation and brilliance of this work founded by 12th century monarchs would not have been possible without the indefatigable continuity of the Cisterican nuns. One faith, one ideal, one habit and one illusion in a group of women dedicated in silence to the cultivation of their high intentions have enabled us today to travel through the long centuries of their activity. Thanks to them this convent is not only a memory. It is still a life.

INDEX